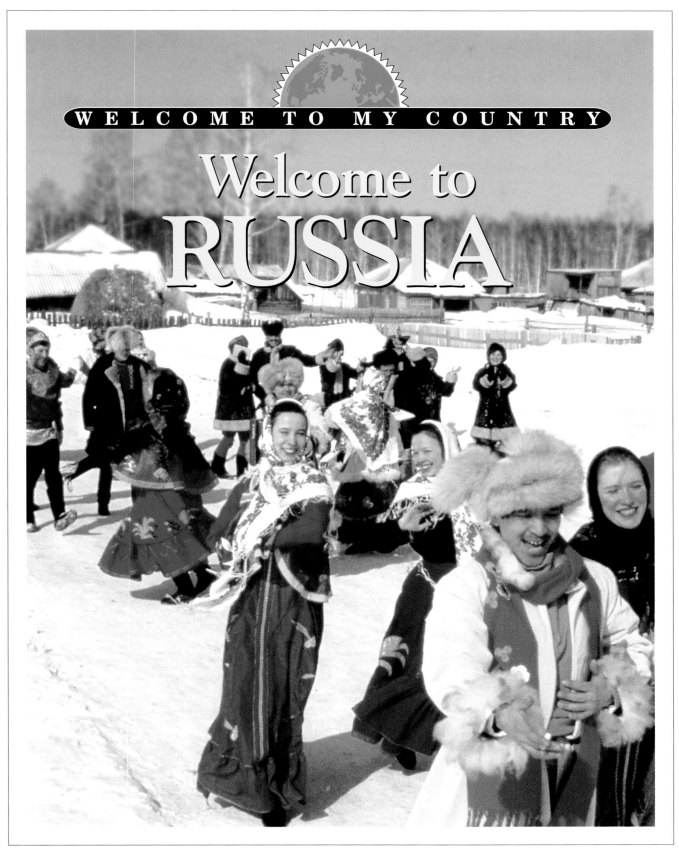

WELCOME TO MY COUNTRY

Welcome to
RUSSIA

Gareth Stevens Publishing
MILWAUKEE

Written by
FIONA CONBOY/TERENCE M. G. RICE

Designed by
LYNN CHIN

Picture research by
SUSAN JANE MANUEL

First published in North America in 2000 by
Gareth Stevens Publishing
1555 North RiverCenter Drive, Suite 201
Milwaukee, Wisconsin 53212 USA

For a free color catalog describing
Gareth Stevens' list of high-quality books
and multimedia programs, call
1-800-542-2595 (USA) or
1-800-461-9120 (CANADA)
Gareth Stevens Publishing's
Fax: (414) 225-0377.

© **TIMES EDITIONS PTE LTD 2000**
Originated and designed by
Times Editions Pte Ltd
Times Centre, 1 New Industrial Road
Singapore 536196
http://www.timesone.com.sg/te

Library of Congress Cataloging-in-Publication Data
Conboy, Fiona.
Welcome to Russia / Fiona Conboy and Terence M. G. Rice
p.   cm. -- (Welcome to my country)
Includes bibliographical references and index.
Summary: An overview of the geography, history, government,
economy, people, and culture of Russia.
ISBN 0-8368-2498-9 (lib. bdg.)
1. Russia (Federation)--Juvenile literature. [1. Russia (Federation)]
I. Rice, Terence M. G. II. Title. III. Series.
DK510.23.C66   2000
947--dc21   99-39898

Printed in Malaysia

1 2 3 4 5 6 7 8 9 04 03 02 01 00

PICTURE CREDITS
Andes Press Agency: 20 (bottom), 41
Bruce Coleman Collection: 3 (center),
   9 (top)
Susanna Burton: 31
Focus Team — Italy: 5, 20 (top), 22, 29,
   30, 34
The Hutchison Library: Cover, 13 (both),
   26, 32 (top)
Liba Taylor Photography: 36 (bottom)
Novosti: 14, 15 (bottom), 32 (bottom), 35,
   38, 40
Novosti (London): 1, 6, 15 (top), 17, 27,
   36 (top), 37, 44
The Society for Cultural Relations with the
   U.S.S.R.: 2, 10, 16, 25
Topham Picturepoint: 3 (bottom), 4,
   9 (bottom), 11, 24, 33
Trip Photographic Library: 3 (top), 7, 8, 12,
   18, 19, 21, 23, 28, 39, 45

Digital Scanning by Superskill Graphics Pte Ltd

Contents

Words that appear in the glossary are printed in **boldface** type the first time they occur in the text.

Welcome to Russia!

Russia, the largest country in the world, is almost twice the size of the United States. Its rich and fascinating history has resulted in an extraordinary mix of European and Asian influences. Despite its troubled past, Russia is now preparing for a bright future. Let's explore Russia and meet its people!

Opposite: Moscow's famous St. Basil's Cathedral is made up of nine churches.

Below: A new generation of Russians is growing up in a young nation.

The Flag of Russia

The Russian flag is made up of white, blue, and red bands. Until 1991, Russia was part of the former Soviet Union, and the flag bore a hammer and sickle on a red background. This signified **revolution** and **communism**.

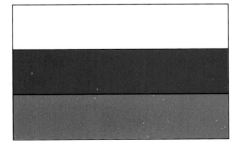

The Land

Covering an area of 6.6 million square miles (17.1 million square kilometers), Russia contains almost every type of geographical feature.

The Ural Mountains run from the deserts of Kazakhstan to the Arctic north. At 18,505 feet (5,640 meters), Mount Elbrus, Russia's highest peak, makes up part of the Caucasus range in southwestern Russia. The Central

Below: The water in Lake Baykal in southern Russia is so pure that it is sold as bottled mineral water.

Russian Upland lies to the south of Moscow. The Central Siberian Plateau in eastern Russia is one of the coldest parts of the country.

Above: The Kamchatka Peninsula, in the far eastern corner of Russia, is home to geysers, hot springs, and volcanoes.

Three of Russia's rivers — the Ob, Yenisey, and Lena — are so wide that when you stand on one bank, you can't see the other side of the river.

No fewer than six seas surround Russia — the Black, Caspian, Baltic, Barents, Okhotsk, and the Sea of Japan.

Seasons

Russia's climate varies dramatically from region to region. During winter in the northern and eastern parts, the temperature falls to as low as -90° Fahrenheit (-68° Celsius)! Summer temperatures, however, soar to about 109° F (43° C) in southern Russia. In the Arctic north, the summer sun does not set for several weeks. This period is called White Nights. Comfortable weather is enjoyed throughout Russia in the spring and autumn months.

Above: The autumn months bring a golden display of leaves.

Plants and Animals

Forests cover large areas of Russia, but in some places in the north, the weather is too extreme for plants to survive. The favorite animal of the Russians is the brown bear, the national mascot. Found mainly in the western forests, it is sometimes called "The Master of the Forests." Antelope, weasels, seals, and many other animals live in Russia, too.

Above: Although the brown bear is Russia's national animal, it is still hunted for its fur.

Left: Red deer are among the many thousands of animal species in Russia.

History

In the ninth century, the Vikings (a people originally from Scandinavia) conquered territories now known as Russia, Ukraine, and Belarus. They called the country *Rus*.

In the thirteenth century, the Mongols from Mongolia invaded and took control of Rus. They ruled the land until the fifteenth century.

Left: In A.D. 988, the Viking ruler Vladimir I was baptized into the Christian church, and Christianity became the official religion of Rus.

National Independence

In the fifteenth century, Viking rulers drove the Mongols out of the land and established national independence for Rus. Ivan IV, later known as Ivan the Terrible, became the first **tsar**. He ruled from 1533 to 1584 and expanded the Russian empire.

In 1613, Tsar Michael Romanov began a dynasty that ruled until 1917. In 1917, rebels forced Nicholas II, Russia's last tsar, to give up the throne.

Above: Between the seventeenth and nineteenth centuries, peasants worked under slave-like conditions for rich landowners. This system was called serfdom. By the late 1800s, rural poverty was widespread, and the people were ready to revolt against their rulers.

Revolution!

The rebels who overthrew the tsar in 1917 set up a parliament, and a minority party called the Bolsheviks took power. Their leader, Vladimir Lenin, was a communist, believing that all people are equal. During the 1920s, the communist Union of Soviet Socialist Republics (U.S.S.R.) — consisting of Russia, Ukraine, Belorussia, and Transcaucasia — was formed.

Above: A 1990 parade in Moscow's Red Square celebrates the rise of communism.

Communism proved difficult to put into practice. Under the rule of Lenin and his successor, Josef Stalin, the U.S.S.R. suffered tremendous social and economic hardship. World War II (1939–1945) also brought heavy losses.

In 1987, a new leader, Mikhail Gorbachev, began to restructure the country and introduce greater freedom. In 1991, the U.S.S.R. broke up to form the Russian Federation and fourteen other independent countries.

Above: This **vandalized** statue of Lenin is a reminder of the difficult years of communist power.

Left: Some Russians still favor communism, as this contemporary display of banners and image of Lenin shows.

Peter the Great (1672–1725)

Peter the Great became tsar at the tender age of seventeen. He spent some time traveling in Western Europe and introduced many **reforms** on his return. As a result, Russia became a powerful nation.

Peter the Great

Catherine the Great (1729–1796)

Catherine II continued the good work Peter the Great had done, and many advances were made during her reign. However, a peasant revolt in 1773 shook the foundations of the empire.

Opposite: Catherine II came to the throne in 1762, when a rebellion forced her husband, Peter III, to abdicate.

Boris Yeltsin (1931–)

After the breakup of the U.S.S.R. in 1991, Boris Yeltsin became the first president of the Russian Federation. Earlier that year, he helped stop a communist revolt against Mikhail Gorbachev by standing on a tank in front of parliament buildings.

Boris Yeltsin

Government and the Economy

After 1917, the Communist Party was the only political party in the U.S.S.R. Mikhail Gorbachev and Boris Yeltsin introduced the reforms that mark the government of today.

In 1993, Russia held its first **democratic** elections. Under the 1993 **constitution**, the president can dissolve parliament.

Below: Since the collapse of communist power, the new democratic government in Russia gives voters more choice.

Parliament

Russia is a democratic republic, with the president as head of state. The parliament is called the Federal Assembly. It consists of the Council of the Federation, which represents the regions, and the State *Duma* (DOO-ma), which has 450 members, each representing a **constituency**. The public votes for members of the Duma in democratic elections.

Above: Members of the State Duma have the power to vote against the government, but the president has the power to disband the Duma, if he disagrees with their decisions.

Natural Resources

Russia is rich in natural resources, such as coal, oil, and gas. During the communist regime, however, the state controlled all industries and did not invest enough money in them. Equipment was not modernized, and methods became outdated. This resulted in a low output from coal mines and oil and gas companies, wasting Russia's plentiful resources.

Above: Russia's forests support growing wood and paper industries.

The Future of Trade and Industry

The long years of communism destroyed the economy of Russia. By the time the Federation was set up in 1991, most industries had been badly affected. A **privatization** process — including the return of land to the peasants — has begun in an effort to rebuild the economy. Today, Russia's trade markets are growing, and its economy is developing toward a healthier future.

Below: Russia imports cars, as well as other luxury goods, from all over the world.

People and Lifestyle

The Russian Federation includes twenty-one republics — it's no wonder that Russia's population is a mix of diverse **ethnic** groups.

Ethnic Russians — people belonging to a group called the East Slavs — make up 85 percent of the population. The remaining 15 percent consists of many different nationalities, including Ukrainians, Belarussians, and Turks.

Above: This man is a member of an ethnic minority. More than seventy ethnic groups live in Russia today.

Left: Young Russian women enjoy a walk in the park.

Urban Life

Life in Russia's towns and cities is very different from that in the countryside. In urban areas, modern shops offer goods from all around the world. Clubs and **societies** provide many opportunities for a busy social life.

Rural life

Most Russians in the countryside make a living from farming and base their working lives around the seasons. Most of them still follow the traditional lifestyles of their ancestors.

Above: The famous GUM department store in Moscow is popular with both locals and tourists.

Family Life

The communist government gave every family a home and everyone a job. However, the standard of housing was sometimes very poor. Although most families earned the same wage, very few could afford luxuries, such as new clothes and children's toys.

Today, there are more opportunities to enjoy some luxuries. The Russian government is selling off industries to

private companies, and people are working hard to build successful careers and businesses.

However, this change has not brought happiness to everyone. Competition for jobs has caused an increase in unemployment, and high property prices have led to overcrowding in the cities. Russia also faces social problems, such as crime, homelessness, and the breakup of families.

Above: Russians value family life. Christmas is an opportunity for the family to spend time together.

School Days

In Russia, children start school at about the age of six. Some attend preschool, where they are taught to read and write, before beginning full-time education. The first eight years of school are required, but most students stay enrolled for at least ten years. Classes are taught six days a week, from Monday to Saturday. The Russian education system is strict and thorough.

Above: Although discipline is an important part of the Russian education system, classes are lots of fun, too!

Higher Education

Competition for acceptance into a university is tough — only about 15 percent of Russians attend universities. Undergraduate degrees take about five years. The Moscow M. V. Lomonosov State University and the St. Petersburg State University are among Russia's most prestigious institutions.

Below: Some students find the pressure of university studies difficult to bear.

Russian Orthodox Christianity

Most Russians practice a religion called Russian Orthodox Christianity. The Rus ruler Vladimir I made Christianity the official religion in the tenth century. When Christianity split into the Orthodox and Catholic faiths in 1054, Russia adopted Orthodox Christianity.

Russian Orthodox beliefs are based on the Bible. The head of the Church is the Patriarch of All Russia.

Below: Priests lead a Russian Orthodox funeral procession.

Other Faiths

Since the breakup of the Soviet Union, Russia has enjoyed greater religious freedom. Muslims are the country's second largest religious group after Orthodox Christians. Buddhism has a small following concentrated near the Caspian Sea and close to the Mongolian border. Jews in Russia were **persecuted** during communist rule and the World Wars. Many of those who survived have since fled the country.

Above: Most Buddhists in Russia live in minority republics.

Language

Russian is Russia's national language. It developed from a Slavic language in the sixth century. Although most ethnic groups use their own languages, they can also speak Russian.

The Russian language uses an alphabet created in the ninth century. It is called the Cyrillic alphabet after one of its creators, Greek monk Cyril. The 33-letter Cyrillic alphabet is based on the Greek alphabet.

Literature

Russia has produced some outstanding writers. Alexander Pushkin is Russia's favorite literary figure. He is known for his colorful, dramatic life, as well as for his splendid written works. Leo Tolstoy's *War and Peace*, set during the

Above: Russians crowd around a busy bookstall in St. Petersburg.

nineteenth century, is one of the longest novels ever written. His work shows remarkable insight into the feelings and behavior of the characters. Anton Chekhov, Russia's most famous playwright, wrote *The Cherry Orchard* and *Uncle Vanya*.

Arts

Russia has contributed great paintings, architecture, and music to world culture during the last nine centuries.

Folk Art

Folk art is still popular in Russia today. Its most famous item is probably the brightly painted *Matriyoshki* (ma-tree-OSH-kee) dolls.

Below: The largest Matriyoshki doll houses a collection of smaller matching dolls, each contained within one another.

Music

Russia's music is as famous as its literature. The nineteenth century produced some of the country's greatest musicians. **Composer** Peter Tchaikovsky created three famous ballets — *The Nutcracker, Swan Lake,* and *Sleeping Beauty.* Other great Russian composers include Nicolai Rimsky-Korsakov and Sergei Rachmaninoff. Their works are appreciated around the world.

Above: A traditional Russian music group performs for passersby. The accordion (*third from left*) is one of Russia's national instruments.

Ballet and Painting

Russia is home to two world-renowned ballet companies — the Bolshoi and the Kirov. They perform before admiring crowds throughout the world.

Above: Russian ballet dancers have always excelled at their art.

Early Russian paintings depicted mainly religious **icons**. During the nineteenth century, **realism**, a technique of portraying people and objects in everyday life, was introduced from Europe.

Left: Two very different architectural styles are represented in these churches in the city of Ivanovo.

Architecture

Moscow's St. Basil's Cathedral, with its nine colorful domes, is a striking example of Russia's early architectural style. Many fortresses and monasteries date from between the eleventh and sixteenth centuries. The biggest change in Russian architecture came about during the 1700s, when the city of St. Petersburg was built. Architects from Holland, Italy, and Germany produced a European-style city.

Opposite: *The Epic Heroes*, by nineteenth-century Russian painter Viktor Vasnetsov, depicts three fourteenth-century Rus warriors.

Leisure

Russians enjoy the same pastimes as many other nationalities. Their vast land and extreme climate make outdoor pursuits, such as hiking, skiing, and fishing, popular. Reading or visiting a gallery are cozier choices in the winter.

Left: Fishing is popular with a few hardy fishermen during the freezing winter months!

Chess

Chess is the one of the most popular games in Russia. Some of the world's best chess champions are from Russia.

Fishing

Fishing is another national favorite — all year round! Despite the freezing temperatures of winter, some eager fishermen make a hole in the ice and wait for a catch.

The Olympic Games

In 1894, Russia was one of the twelve countries that decided to revive the Olympic Games. Russia has competed successfully ever since, both as part of the U.S.S.R. and, in 1996, as an independent nation.

Russia's most successful Olympic sport is gymnastics. Soviet gymnast

Larissa Latynina holds the record as winner of the most Olympic gold medals (eighteen). Since the recent reforms, many of Russia's athletes have become professionals — a status not allowed under communism.

Below: A troika ride is a fast way to travel in the snow!

The Troika

Russians enjoy an unusual form of horse racing called the *troika* (TROY-ka). A troika is a sleigh pulled by a team of three horses. Troika rides have become popular with tourists.

Holidays

Religious celebrations were banned during communist rule. Today, however, the Christian holidays of Christmas and Easter, the Muslim festival of **Ramadan**, and the Jewish **Yom Kippur** are enjoyed once more. Shrovetide is a popular Christian holiday at the beginning of Lent.

The highlight of Shrovetide celebrations is feasting on delicious *bliny* (BLEE-nee), or small pancakes.

The ethnic groups in Russia enjoy their holidays, as well. Navruz (nahv-ROOZ) is a Muslim festival that marks the coming of spring. The festival of *Sabantui* (sah-bant-OOEH) celebrates the sowing of crops in springtime. Its name comes from *saban*, meaning "plow," and *tui*, meaning "celebration."

Below: Dancers wear colorful costumes at a Sabantui festival.

Food

Due to its interesting ethnic mix, Russia offers a wonderful variety of food. Influences from Europe and Asia have enhanced traditional Russian dishes. City restaurants serve food from around the world.

A typical Russian meal starts with rye bread and appetizers, known as **zakuski** (ZAK-oos-kee). A warming vegetable soup, called *shchi* (shee),

follows. The main course usually consists of meat or fish on plates piled high with hearty vegetables. Black tea and delicious, spicy candies end the meal.

Bliny

Bliny is Russia's national dish. The small, light pancakes can be eaten as an appetizer or as a meal in themselves with sour cream and Russian **caviar**.

RUSSIA

Legend:
- State Boundary
- ■ Capital
- ● City
- River
- Republic Boundary
- 16 Republic

ARCTIC OCEAN

BARENTS SEA

SEVERNAYA ZEMLYA

NEW SIBERIAN ISLAND

NOVAYA ZEMLYA

SWEDEN

FINLAND

BALTIC SEA

ESTONIA

Kaliningrad

LATVIA

LITHUANIA

St. Petersburg

BELARUS

Kiev

MOSCOW

Ivanovo

Central Russian Upland

Kazan

Volga

UKRAINE

URAL MOUNTAINS

West Siberian Plain

Ob

Yenisey

Central Siberian Plateau

SIBERIA

BLACK SEA

Mt. Elbrus (18,505 feet/ 5,640m)

CAUCASUS

GEORGIA

ARMENIA

AZERBAIJAN

CASPIAN SEA

Novosibirsk

Lake Baykal

KAZAKHSTAN

TURKMENISTAN

UZBEKISTAN

KYRGYZSTAN

TAJIKISTAN

CHINA

MONGOLIA

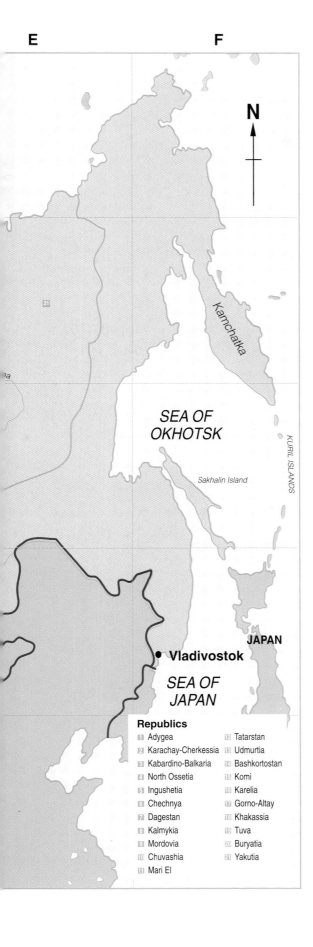

E   F

N

SEA OF
OKHOTSK

Kamchatka

KURIL ISLANDS

Sakhalin Island

JAPAN

● Vladivostok

SEA OF
JAPAN

Republics

1	Adygea	12	Tatarstan
2	Karachay-Cherkessia	13	Udmurtia
3	Kabardino-Balkaria	14	Bashkortostan
4	North Ossetia	15	Komi
5	Ingushetia	16	Karelia
6	Chechnya	17	Gorno-Altay
7	Dagestan	18	Khakassia
8	Kalmykia	19	Tuva
9	Mordovia	20	Buryatia
10	Chuvashia	21	Yakutia
11	Mari El		

Arctic Ocean A1–F1
Armenia A4
Azerbaijan A4

Baltic Sea A2
Barents Sea B1–C1
Baykal, Lake D4
Belarus A2
Black Sea A4

Caspian Sea A4
Caucasus
    Mountains A4
Central Russian
    Upland A3
Central Siberian
    Plateau D2
China C5–E4

Estonia A2

Finland A2–B1

Georgia A4

Ivanovo A2

Japan F4

Kazakhstan B4
Kazan B3
Kiev (Ukraine) A3

Latvia A2
Lena River E2
Lithuania A2

Mongolia D4
Moscow A2
Mt. Elbrus A4

Novosibirsk C4

Ob River C3

Sea of Japan F4
Sea of Okhotsk F3
Siberia (region) D3
St. Petersburg A2
Sweden A1

Turkmenistan
    A4–B5

Ukraine A2–A3
Ural Mountains B3
Uzbekistan A4–B5

Vladivostok F4
Volga River B3

West Siberian
    Plain C3

Yenisey River C3

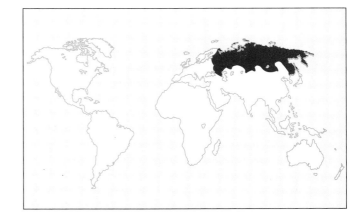

Quick Facts

Official Name   Russia; the Russian Federation

Capital   Moscow

Official Language   Russian

Population   148 million (1998 estimate)

Land Area   6.6 million square miles (17.1 million sq. km)

Republics   Adygea, Bashkortostan, Buryatia, Chechnya, Chuvashia, Dagestan, Gorno-Altay, Ingushetia, Kabardino-Balkaria, Kalmykia, Karachay-Cherkessia, Karelia, Khakassia, Komi, Mari El, Mordovia, North Ossetia, Tatarstan, Tuva, Udmurtia, Yakutia

Highest Point   Mt. Elbrus at 18,505 feet (5,640 m)

Major Rivers   Don 1,160 miles (1,867 km)

Ob 3,362 miles (5,411 km, including the Irtysh)

Volga 2,193 miles (3,529 km)

Yenisey 2,540 miles (4,088 km)

Major Religion   Russian Orthodox Christianity

Important Holidays   New Year (January 1)

Orthodox Christmas (January 7)

National Day (June 12)

Currency   Ruble (23.4 rubles = U.S. $1 in 1999)

Opposite: A large Soviet mural in St. Petersburg depicts the Russian people.

Glossary

abdicate: to formally give up power.

caviar: the salted eggs of a large fish, such as a sturgeon.

communism: the theory or practice of basing a society on equality and on the common ownership of property. Communism was first written about by German philosopher Karl Marx.

composer: a person who writes music.

constituency: an electoral district.

constitution: the basic principles and laws of a nation.

democratic: describes a system of government in which power rests with the people, who elect their governing representatives.

Duma (DOO-ma)**:** the Russian state assembly, or state council.

ethnic: describes a group of people with a common language and culture.

icons: religious images usually featured on painted panels.

Matriyoshki (ma-tree-OSH-kee) **dolls:** brightly painted wooden dolls contained inside one another.

persecuted: made to suffer for beliefs, values, background, or origin.

privatization: the act of selling a government-owned organization to a private, profit-making company.

Ramadan: the ninth month of the Muslim year, celebrated with daily fasting from dawn until dusk.

realism: in art, the representation of objects as they are in life.

reforms: improvements made by removing faults.

revolution: the overthrow of a government by its people.

societies: groups organized around shared hobbies, interests, or other social activities.

troika (TROY-ka)**:** a Russian sleigh, or carriage, pulled by three horses.

tsar: emperor; the ruler of Russia until 1917.

vandalized: describes private or public property that was deliberately destroyed or damaged.

Yom Kippur: a Jewish festival celebrated in October or November with fasting and prayer.

zakuski (ZAK-oos-kee)**:** tasty appetizers, such as bliny served with caviar.

More Books to Read

Ancient Horsemen of Siberia. Time Travelers series. Janet Buell (Millbrook Press)

Moscow. World 100 Years Ago series. Burton Holmes (Chelsea House Publishing)

Russia. Eyewitness Books series. Kathleen Berton Murrell and Andy Crawford (Knopf)

Russia. Festivals of the World series. Harlinah Whyte (Gareth Stevens)

Russia: Building Democracy. Topics in the News series. John Bradley (Raintree/Steck-Vaughn)

Russia. Nations in Transition series. Michael Kort (Facts on File)

Russia: New Freedoms, New Challenges. Exploring Cultures of the World series. Virginia Schomp (Benchmark Books)

St. Petersburg. Cities of the World series. Deborah Kent (Children's Press)

Videos

Discovering Russia. (Ivn Entertainment)

The Faces of Russia. (Home Vision Cinema)

Leo Tolstoy's Anna Karenina. (Warner Studios)

War and Peace. (Twentieth Century Fox)

Web Sites

www.alincom.com/russ

www. pbs.org/weta/faceofrussia

russia.uthsosa.edu

www.russia.com

Due to the dynamic nature of the Internet, some web sites stay current longer than others. To find additional web sites about Russia, use a reliable search engine and enter one or more of the following keywords: *Mikhail Gorbachev, Vladimir Lenin, Moscow, Peter the Great, Russia, serfs, Slavic, Leo Tolstoy, Boris Yeltsin.*

Index